EXTRAORDINARY FORMS

Also by Joy Howard from Grey Hen

SECOND BITE
(with Hilary J Murray and Gina Shaw)

EXIT MOONSHINE

Edited by Joy Howard at Grey Hen

A TWIST OF MALICE

CRACKING ON

NO SPACE BUT THEIR OWN

GET ME OUT OF HERE!

THE PRICE OF GOLD

RUNNING BEFORE THE WIND

TRANSITIONS

OUTLOOK VARIABLE

SHADES OF MEANING

From Ward Wood Publishing

REFURBISHMENT

EXTRAORDINARY FORMS

Some wonders of the natural world

Edited by Joy Howard

Illustrations: Sue Harvey Dawson

First published in 2016 by Grey Hen Press
PO Box 450
Keighley
West Yorkshire
BD22 9WS
www.greyhenpress.com

Printed by Flexpress, Birstall Leicester LE4 3BY

Endless forms most beautiful and most wonderful have been and are being evolved.

Charles Darwin

Contents

Prologue

Mammaliana

Beaks and Feathers

Cold Blood

Creepies and Crawlies

Us and Them

Endpiece

Prologue

Species

Sometimes they rise before me in the night,
the lemurs, eyes as bare and bright as moons,
the lizard, older than the afternoon,
the coral's tender hands which sun bleached white.
Some are immense, the tiger, shot and still,
some thumbnail-sized, like Chile's emerald frog
I never saw, and soon, nobody will.

Alison Brackenbury

Mammaliana

Poverty Pig

Dusk over Jasper County, and here
he comes, old Dazypus, the nocturnal
plodder, snuffling past us on the road
towards Hampton. Small Armoured
One, they've called him, Azotochtli,
Hoover Hog, but the names do not
concern him. Unhurried, stopping
only to sniff the air or forage verges
with snout and claws, he stuffs in ants
grubs, beetles, tubers, the occasional
frog, with just a flick of the tongue.
The journey's been a long one, from
the rainforests, across the Isthmus,
the Rio Grande, Texas, Florida, through
their swamps, scrublands and prairies,
leaving a trail of fusty burrows. Now we
watch him as he heads up to Kentucky,
Nebraska, Illinois - and look, he can put on
a turn of speed if needed, has learnt this
trick of jumping three or four feet high
should trouble threaten. At such times
it's a toss-up who will come off worse,
Dasypus novemcinctus or Homo Sapiens,
those good ol' boys hollering after him
in battered pickups and rusty Chevys.

Angela Kirby

Walking Whales

They talk underwater, listen through gaps
in massive jawbones. If you dip
an ear to the river in the midday silence,
thunderwaves vibrate up and down
the Limpopo, high pitched squeals, vuvuzelas,
Grandad's long snore, the rattle of false teeth,
a man's cry at the moment of ejaculation,
underscored by sharp sonar clicks.

On the surface, only a twitch of grey nostrils
an occasional wheeze, a slow spew of bubbles.
They seem funny as fat frogs, except, rising
up from the muddy water at dusk,
to gorge themselves on grass, you see old scars,
deep fresh wounds.

Eveline Pye

Black Velvet

You curse me. I ruin your careful course,
earth-mound your close drained grass.
Blind, I know your goings and comings,
hear soil pounded by hoof and foot.

Which of you has seen me?
I am sharp-toothed darkness,
the narrowness of earth that soon
must claim your tawdry light.

Pauline Kirk

Monkey

It's been over a year since he perched on the jeep's windshield.
Handsome bugger. Grey langur, though he looks more gold
                                                    to me.
And all he's come for is to say 'Up yours!'

Not the alpha male, I'd say. More like a trusted minion
sent to annoy with a message of pure disdain. Handsome,
though, like he's had his hair done at Vidal Sassoon's.

Nice layered look. Arms, tum, bum, the same.
(Paraffin foot wax? Deluxe manicure?)
This guy knows he looks so-o-o-o-o good...

He gets bored with looking down on us, bounds through the jeep,
shitting all the way. Smooth black hands, feet, face, flying.
Handsome bugger. Tiger food. Better him than me.

Anne Stewart

9

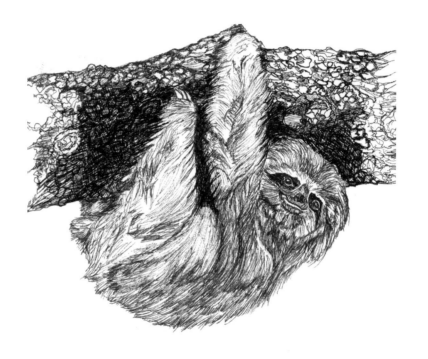

Suspended

each scene upturned
three toes clinging
shifting slowly
inch by lingering inch
along the leaf-lined ceiling
where time stands still
a face briefly seen
bitumen eyes and
Mona Lisa smile
another inch is travelled
captured in slow motion
then wearied by the day
the somnolent sloth
still suspended
slowly
slothfully
slumbers

Sylvia Fairley

Ice Bears

Were you aware
that polar bears
deceive the sight
in seeming white?

The truth is, their
translucent hairs
are quills that fill
with distilled light.

Stevie Krayer

Up Tree Down

Out from under
spiky juniper
peeps
      now jumping
         (so young)
      now running
        pause
        now

               m   e   r
          o   s
        s   a
         g   u
       n   l
        i   t

      now
      p a u s i n g
      (look at me
       in my white and tan)
running up tree
   d
    o
     w
      n

         t
        r
         e
           e

all around tree
back under
      juniper
         runs
         weasel . . .

Vee Singleton

Beaks and Feathers

Bowerbird

He made a rainbow on the forest floor;
a flounce of flowers, coloured stones, small flags
of shining rag; paper, berries, foil -
with him in his outlandish finery,
dancing attention, drawing her in.

His song, translated, said:
I've made all this for you, my flighty dear;
a bower so beautiful
you'll never want to leave.
Come be my love, live with me here.

She stood bedazzled by the door,
this small grey bird, and as he danced,
allowed his twice-told tales to fill her ear.
She tried his nest for size,
and was entranced.

He brought no more bright stones.
Instead he kept the world away.
Be dutiful, it's all for your own good,
she heard him say.

When hours, days, weeks had passed
and with them all her chicks,
her hopes, his song, she fluttered
- shook him off the way a dog shakes water;
caught the flare of flowers in the sun, was gone.

Ann Alexander

17

Cassowary

Behemoth of the bird world, veloceraptor,
Left behind in the race for flight.
Tiny wings, no steer bones, ungainly body -
You're a laughing stock, a charmless sight.
Stumps for legs, unwieldy ostrich feet.
Wedge shaped headgear - floor sweeper, forage tool,
Sound box casque - booming your call through trees.
Rainbow bib on your black hair feathers,
Neon glare under your hooked beak.
Yellow pupils hostile in your brown-eyed stare.
Evolution wasn't kind. Yet you can run,
swim and nearly jump your height, triathlon style.
Best kept secret, your three-toed feet hide
A killer weapon: that murderous dagger
In your middle claw. Rainforest guardian,
We get the message. You are no pushover.

Rosemary Doman

Fish Crow

Six thirty. Faint daylight sieved
through rusting screens
seeps onto beds.
Then the bulky black fish crow
from his office in the palm tree
announces that night is done.
Ca-Ha! Ca-Ha!
His nasal, grouchy mariner's injunction
torpedoes through our darkened heads.
A caustic, hoarse, knowing call
fretfully agreeing with itself.
Oh, yes. Ca-Ha! Ca-Ha!
Gutteral, grating, remorseless broadcast.
Querulous Ca-Ha! Ca-Ha!
Until lights snap on in windows,
coffee makers burble.
Next-door truck never starts first time
but barks, engine gagging,
stutters to action, rolls away
to the ice plant, hurling dust.
Only then does the scurrilous bird
flap off towards the tidewater
to forage. Obligation discharged.

Jenny Morris

Black Owl
(in South Africa)

We step off the track
and see the round cat-faced
prick-eared owl, body bent

like a bundle of feathered twigs
nesting in the roots of a tree
so dark it might have grown

from her own heart. How do I know
her feet are black? Her mate stands
still as the spring from a stopped watch

his obsidian feet stapled to a branch.
Her eyes, stringent as iodine, teach
how proper distance is the hardest shore
to reach.

Kate Foley

Bad Day at the Office

Red-eyed after a heavy night
the Secretary Bird
has put his knees on back to front
and wildly overdone the hair gel

Best not cross his path today
if taken for a rat or a snake
man are you gonna get stomped on

Joy Howard

Doubletake

Mindfuck you call it – technically,
cognitive dissonance. First, the place,
a cottage garden hugging the moorland path,
where he shudders as he beats the bounds,
spinning his fantail like a disco-ball,
wafting with shapely feathers an indifferent peahen,
his urgent hoarseness the solo
to a backing track of curlews and larks.
          She's unimpressed – seen it before –
but look again – no turquoise eye
is shimmering on a bronzed plume.
Perhaps the Pennine rain has bled him dry
for every feather's innocent of tint,
and like the sky's broad colourchart of greys
so he displays each variant of white,
of clouds, of cottongrass, of milk,
spume rising from the stream
or mist plunging down from the hillside.
          He's trembling, striving to keep it up:
still he gyrates, still she ignores
his desperate pride, the hunger
for her plump, ordinary brownness.

Hannah Stone

Blue-Footed Booby
(Sequence showing plunge diving)

Top of climb
You have captured gravity
wings outstretched,
hanging like a comma
in a paused sky.

Still Point
All your creature parts
retract, tighten, stream,
trailing edges grey-splayed
riffling with lift.

Earth Tilt
Your feet, belly-tucked, etched
like sky stain underwing,
you turn beak down and
gravity breaks free.

Dive
Filaments slick
with slipstream
feather tips
spilling sky
every sinew
a trajectory
an impossible
equation
of falling
into your
own
furrow
of
air.

Plunge
You slip between
your elements, flesh
a hiss of oxygen.
White crown of ocean rises.

disappears.

Deborah Sloan

Note: title taken from Wikipedia page on Blue-Footed Booby but the poem is
inspired by the author's own photo sequence of the bird.

Cold Blood

Amoeboid

One cell, no eyes,
all sides. My coastline
flows like the sea's edge.
I'm a creature of tides,

my own tiny moon.
I could be swallowed,
unnoticed, in a glass of water
or live forever

in my own terms.
You cannot get inside.
I am one, inviolate,
a shifting, coherent

whole. Adrift in a sea
of sharks and foam,
jellyfish and manta rays,
sky-blacking whales

and tiny luminescent beings.
I am one. The year dot.
A little zero full of light
and life. My own home.

Fiona Durance

Shinglebacks

Down under, the ugliest lizards in the world
drag their bodies and thick broad tails along
the scrubland. Like a length of scaly conifer branch
with stumpy legs, they go slow. Slow.

But wait. They mate for life, the male trundling
behind his love. One narrow boat towing another.
She struggles like any mother's daughter to push out
her young, two or three, head first.

And when in a roaring cloud of dust a truck wheel
runs over a lazy lizard, which happens often,
its mate will stay for hours by the corpse,
nudging it gently, waiting for life to resume.

Jean Watkins

Watching Grass Snakes

She was looped
on a pallet of reeds
hunting for marsh frogs
when he swam
in one straight line,
pipped like a domino,
black on lime green,
pouring onto the bank
and over the reeds
in an urgent ripple
to thrust through her
dull olive folds. Together
they stiffened and thrashed
like a rope – then stayed
entwined, flicking
their blue-black tongues,
as the water slopped
and lifted the reeds.

Then he left her, coiling
away, head raised
eeling along the stream,
a flash of yellow
at his neck, his body
snakier than hers,
primed for another
ecstatic figure of eight
before the drought set in
and life disappeared
from the unsustainable marsh.

Ruth Smith

Salmo salar

She hangs in the autumn water,
a kite in her element
tugged by river-wind.

Her nose searches the currents
for scents of the gravel bed
where she became.

That spring remembered
when she pushed from her redd,
between boulders

as big as her alevin self.
Through the massacre
of frogs, trout, herons

she has transformed:
fry, then parr, then her smolt-self
sucks salt, slips from her natal stream;

grows as an ocean grilse, wary
of seals, sharks, skate, cod
till, belly fat with three thousand lives,

she snouts out that stream,
fans and writhes in a cloud of milt
over this river gravel.

Now kelt, exhausted,
she turns through the bodies
of dying cock fish,

her hunger pulling her
back to the salt,
the salt.

Char March

33

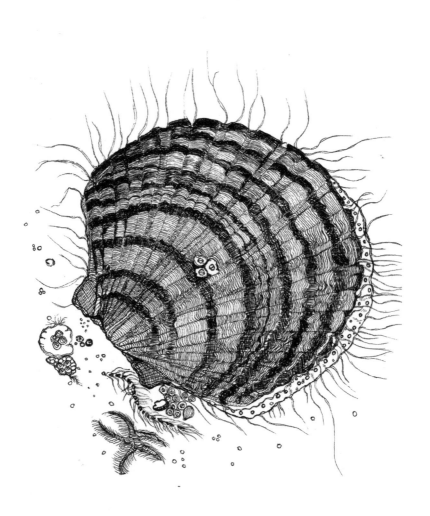

Queen of the Sea

Some things they will not eat, the perfect ones;
nothing with soft fur, nothing with arms and legs,
nothing with handly paws that reach and touch.
Nothing with eyes.

But for the soft queen in her pilgrim-shell
there is no argument. No dispensation.
They sear her flesh, consume her tawny sex;
she's thing, not animal.

They do not understand the secret eyes
scattered like pearls along the frilly hem
of her flouncing petticoat as she dances,
dances, or know that they are blue.

Ann Drysdale

Amphibian Love-song

We hear you more than a mile away
Revving up your stretched-elastic song,
A thousand voices with the timbre
Of a rubbed balloon.
Above them all I hear my darling,
My own handsome spadefoot, garlic-scented,
Buzzing with lust, chest puffed proud,
In this day's new-minted pool
In the broiling desert of Arizona,
Beneath a smiling moon.

I will shovel free from my cool coffin
To swarm with the urgent, ripe females
Who converge now on your maleness
Like an imploding star. And there
You are – the water thrutching with expectation.
You find me.
And as your foreleg slips around my waist,
My eggs slither down.
Tomorrow we will feed and part.
All year I will listen for your call.

Frances Nagle

Frilled Lizard

You may think
   he's hungry for crickets
      and that's why

he's tapping
   the vivarium glass
      with his delicate claw.

But you'd be wrong.
   Go on – slide open
      the door –

place your finger
   under his pouchy jaw.
      Try it! Tickle his skin,

watch how he settles,
   how he curves his mouth
      into a blissful grin.

No, there's no need
   to wear gloves –
      he won't put up a fight

he may be cold to the touch
   but inside
      he's alight.

Maggie Sawkins

Creepies and Crawlies

A Woman's Work

Look at her up there, Teggy Domesticus, in her
sooty leotard and four black pairs of sequined tights.

How nimbly she points her toes, spins a thread
from one end of the curtain pole, swings with it

up to the picture rail in the corner. She's perfecting
her art. It's mirrored in her tiara eyes. I'm sure

she could weave her web blindfold, create the most
elegant eight-sided dinner plate. Her hatchlings

emerge from their eggs holding the pattern
in their heads. But first they must learn to side step

the early circus of a multi-coloured feather duster
or a bumble bee stumbling in from the garden

into a minor inconvenience. It'll soon pull free
and buzz off, leaving her web in tatters again.

Pat Borthwick

Lumbricus rex

Upon my belly I shall go, proudly. A stately retinue
unto myself, no hole or palace barred me, I shall proceed
at ease through private studded corridors – or else
encased in grit, shall lie with it, pulsing, rippling, alive.

At once tongue, finger, penis, nipple – what more is there?
My soul a gut, I shall have more yet: my own self to love,
my kind to meet and feed at death – but, half immortal,
each thrill of heat, dust, ice and flood till then to taste,
more dazzled by their spectrum than by sensed space or light.

Seismically tuned, my body's length a flexible antenna,
time, too, will be mine to apprehend. Lowest of the low,
knowing salvation and damnation, I shall fear nothing.
Bow down, world, to me. I shall be god of earth.

Julia Deakin

Snail
Excerpt from 'Dunstanburgh'

From a hole in the seaward wall, a snail
Stretches its foreparts, eases its tail,

Oozing over the knobbly grain,
Smoothing the stone with its slimy trail.

Its skirts slacken under it. Stretching one eye
To examine a patch of leafy lichen,

It feels its way down a ribbon of silver,
Studded with seashells, ancient mortar,

Fossil of top-shell, cowrie, lime
Sliding under it. Taking its time.

Its slow mouth working, its gluey strings
Trembling in the breeze like skin,

It slithers over root and stalk
And crevice, the sepulchral dark

Hollow of the sea wall, where
The empty shell's reoccupied –

Invisible creatures twitch inside
An alabaster palace, made

In a single movement, from the twist
Of its newel post to its silky lip,

And everything circular starts again.

Katrina Porteous

A Worm Updates Itself

Never mind the Tree of Knowledge:
I'd sooner get my teeth into a book, or
better still a row – complete works
from long ago, not bleached or sized.
Give me the tender wrap of calves shaved thin,
a volume in a warm damp room, its spine
relaxed in fishy corrugations. I've delved
into the great minds of the past, chewed over
their hypotheses, digested fantasies
and left behind a dust sucked dry of thought.

But things are harder now: I crack
my head on plastic, slip on silicon.
Yet I'll survive – I've found a way
to tunnel the soft underside of 0 and 1.

Gill Learner

Flickering

Last night I didn't see
a firefly.
I saw
the light,
the spark, the blink,
the dot and dash,
the morse -
that mini-sem-
aphore that spells
out
in winks:
Love – me! Love –
me!
The night
was dark as mines, hot as
C° thirty-nine. My
fire-
fly jittered, got
unscrewed, went out,
stopped
signalling on the night
Love –
me! Love – me! Bet
it had met a
firefly mate and
quick as
lightning on the
moon
had found
love's batteries soon run out
on the ground.

Gabriel Griffin

A Hairy Caterpillar Talks to God

So. This is what you're saying...my skin,
my cosy furry skin, will split?
no clever-stitched episiotomy,
but out of control, ragged, jagged
starting first here, then higher,

the swollen inside forcing its way through
all gold-green quivering, barely solid;
still the hollow shapes of stumps
where once I had legs.

And I will have no use for legs?

Have to pierce a nettle leaf,
trust the dark, hang there, my body
hardening leaf-brown, unnoticed

while my inside liquefies. Disintegration soup,
where I have no choice, allowed no comfort
even in distant memory, of summer evenings
holding lavender shimmer in wings of glass.

I just hope You know what you're talking about.

Sheila Templeton

Foundling

The eggs were a gift I had not asked for,
a cluster of translucent pinheads in a tube
from which you emerged too early, before Christmas,
no bigger than a lime-green eyelash, the wisp
of horn on your tail already visible.

For two months I have crammed your cage
with offerings of privet. You eat and grow
relentlessly, as if you really are on the baked plains
of central Europe, resting from the sun
above the clinker of your dark droppings.

It is snowing again; I have to knock blizzards
from branches, pat each leaf dry. You reward me
with a fifth moult, swelling inside
your stretched skin until it splits,
until you lie beside the rucked-up debris

glistening, freshly painted: seven purple chevrons
straddling two shades of green, rows
of spiracles like portholes, your new horn
thicker, yellow as a stamen
clotted with pollen. You are already

three inches long, and perfect.
I mark each instar with a thrill
of apprehension, watching the mercury fall
to zero, waking to frost and you feeding greedily
by the radiator. I would give everything

to see you break out of your pupa, everything
for you never to; will not be able to tear
my eyes away as your wings fill and harden
and the skull and crossed bones unfold
on your thorax like a premonition –

nor delay the moment of letting you go
into a raw English night as if I believe
you will survive, that our woods are massed
with hawkmoths flexing their spans, shuddering
like leaves among the leafless trees.

Caroline Price

Us and Them

Golden Lion Tamarins
Mata Atlântica, Brazil

We are dexterous children
dripped from the sun.
Fire on the run,
our AC current
busy in the trees.

We shimmer, shine:
we are jacinth and wine.
Lithe fingers, long tails,
a sinuous line.

Light in suspension
as if an artist
stalled, stood back;
an alchemist,
astonished.

Hear us at play –
Zee-zee-zee! Our
bird-notes fill the canopies.
Their green looms quiver

as chainsaws quicken.
They keen, drone,
carve beauty to bone,
forests to islands.

Dark eyes, lit manes:
our gold-rimmed mirrors
echo your gaze –

a dance of light
in the pupils' glaze –

sun-shoed and gone.

Lynne Wycherley

The Atlântica rainforest, lion tamarins' only habitat, has
been reduced to fragments

53

A Question of Balance

Centred in a ring of lights, attached
by electrodes to a Swiss robot,
the lamprey's brain turns to the light

(its first function overwritten -
to keep its owner upright
in the vast salt tideflow)

If one of the robot's eyes is masked
the brain becomes confused
but quickly learns to adjust

while on the other side of the world
a human brain, disrupted by some neural
accident, waits to discover

whether this patch, snipped
from one edge of the universe
can mend a hole elsewhere

It is a miracle
but the lamprey in its cool salt fluid
rich with oxygen, turning

obediently from light to light, wonders
where all the dark has gone
where all the dark has gone

Christine Webb

Ballenisles

A residential community in Florida

How deceptively it rhymes
with crocodiles
when in truth, it is alligators
cruise these lagoons --

alligators, slick and silent
who rattle past double-gate,
triple-guard security:
uniformed figures
behind tinted glass,
backed by cell phones, hand guns,
the full weight
of the law.

Iron-spiked fences
protect children and pets
but not from Coragyps Atratus, –
those clumsy scavengers,
who flail their tattered wings
feed on carrion, eat eggs,
kill new-borns.

No one is safe from attack
in Ballenisles
from creatures
who lay their eggs
in caves or hollow trees,
who slither at speed
at a glimpse of a child at play
on the wrong side of a fence,
at a dog with a ball;

no one is safe from predators
who are urban,
suburban, bucolic,
who may breed
under the shadow bars of palm fronds,
who are never far off.

Wendy Klein

Snow Leopard on Film

point that thing at me all you like
you can't see me
I am
dirty snow and black basalt
I am eyes of ice and sky
I am deadly
weight and flash of tooth
and muscle and claw
and fur

I know you're there
across the singing water
I smell you, flesh and metal and
            almost-fear

I twitch my ear
(markhor hooves clattering down)
but you won't see its black flick
till I'm gone
I bunch
tense
balance tail
now
dash down
onrush of fur
            down
parting the thin air
            down
to the singing water
to the kill

now you see me
because I allow it

Mandy Macdonald

My Tiger

My tiger, in her portrait, pauses mid-pace on grass,
behind her the tropical dark; her heavy, handsome head
turned to appraise the lens, exhibits, model-style,
her whiskered chops just parted, pink tongue peeping,
and the alien gold eyes in a full-on stare.

Beautiful, my Kamrita. I have a stake in her -
monthly I stow away in a banker's draft,
fleet above wide oceans, mountain ranges, deserts,
come to my great cat sleeping, caress her massy paw,
stroke sparks from the smooth nap of her splendid side.

Fooled? – is this only a donor-charming scam -
the cash buys fence-posts, stun-guns, desert-rovers,
wages for sweating lads in tattered shorts?
'Kamrita' a catch-all name – she's everybody's,
handy composite image, striped fund-raiser?

What if? For me still, slack in her rich, loose skin,
she sleeps, shields me in the crook of a warm foreleg.
Her clean-cat smell, her purring sigh, her warmth, transport me
also to sleep, in a dappling forest of bright birdsong,
of whispering monkeys, under a million leaves.

Alison Edwards

The Elephant

Elephants were not her cup of tea –
they were mammoth and boring,
immobile, they turned no somersaults.
Gaiety and the antics of monkeys
and insulting parakeets,
blinking and chattering,
offered her the warmth of fur and vivid feathers.
Elephants were distant, tusked and ominous.
Powerful and towering over children,
their long memories and wisdom
placed them in a different zoo – for adults.
'But this is an Indian elephant,'
her father said. 'It is homesick
and will cheer up to see an Indian girl
in this wet, cold, foreign land.'
So she tore away from the noisy cages
and allowed herself to be slowly led
to greet her majestic compatriot.
She avoided those massive tree trunk legs
and looked straight up at the eyes.
A storehouse of sorrow was locked in its brain.
Tentative, she reached out and patted
the incredible trunk stretched out to her.

Debjani Chatterjee

Buffalo

I went to the zoo and sat by a fence,
right near the head of a sleeping buffalo,
I sat there for a long time while he slept.

His head was massive, warm and heavy.
He shuffled a little in his sleep.
I sat by him until I was still as a prairie and wide.

He showed me some mystery and wildness
and that he still had his dreams.

Rose Cook

The Urbane Gorilla

Where we eat we're also on display
and here you are to look. I'm used to that.
If I crash huffing to the ground
and cuff my sister it is part for show,
and part so she should understand priority.
I eat first. Do stay. I like a chat.
If I didn't I would take my lunch and go.
There are places we can have our privacy.
I could vanish in the spirals of the climbing dome,
or walk the field that stretches down below
with follies, ha-has, an expanse of lawn.
We are a well-to-do community.

You think we are shut in? I don't agree.
We keep intruding visitors at bay
with fences. You'd be sitting on my straw
helping yourself to what there was to snack,
your children shinning up my tower
without these boundaries, I suspect.
Freedom has its limits. Once you call
a place a home you have something to protect.
If I drew a line to show your passage
through an ordinary day would you not go
round and round a fairly beaten track?
It's often so.

Sometimes, you people ask if I feel torn,
missing hot forests where I spent
my youth. Odd question. I was born
not far from here, in Kent.
In the thick of dreams it's true, I push through trees
where ripe fruit falls into my hands, the air
steaming, dense, the sky deep blue.
But then, there's not a soul who doesn't hold
the myth of some lost Eden deep inside him.
Even you.

Melanie Penycate

Endpiece

Dreaming the Ancestor

something's climbing out of the sea
legs barely able to support its body

later it will go back   become a whale

but my dream always takes me further up the family tree
fogged by shifting clouds
aeons   light years
till I come to a creature
deciphered from archeological fragments
four-legged   shapeless   inert

and it's lying on its side like a dog that's run too many miles
and it's lying on its side as if weary of the idea of becoming
                                                    human
and it's lying on its side because it wants to turn round and
                                                    go back

Caroline Carver

The Poets

Ann Alexander has three collections of poetry, and a fourth on the way. She has won first prize in the Grey Hen, Bedford Open, Mslexia and Frogmore poetry competitions.

Pat Borthwick lives in the East Riding of Yorkshire where fortunately poems still beat their way to her door in a remote hamlet on top of the chalky Wolds.

Alison Brackenbury's latest collection is *Then* (Carcanet, 2013). Her ninth collection will be published by Carcanet in Spring 2016. New poems can be read at: www.alisonbrackenbury.co.uk

Rose Cook has had three collections of her poetry published. Her latest is *Notes from a Bright Field* (Cultured Llama Publishing 2013). She lives in Devon. www.rosecook.wordpress.com

Caroline Carver is a National Poetry Prize winner, poet-in-residence with the Marine Institute, Plymouth University, a Hawthornden Fellow, and currently working on her sixth collection. She lives in Cornwall.

Debjani Chatterjee has been called 'Britain's best-known Asian poet' (Elisabetta Marino) and 'a national treasure' (Sixties Press), with over 65 books for children and adults.
www.debjanichatterjee.moonfruit.com

Julia Deakin has written three highly-praised collections: *The Half-Mile-High Club, Without a Dog* and *Eleven Wonders*. Widely published, she has won many competitions and appeared on *Poetry Please*.

Rosemary Doman is a retired tutor in creative writing and English, who writes poetry and short stories. She has been published in various anthologies and magazines and had success in writing competitions.

Ann Drysdale has published five poetry collections, as well as memoir, essays and a gonzo guidebook to the City of Newport. She lives in a mining town in South Wales.

Fiona Durance's writing has featured in many magazines and anthologies, in theatres, galleries and on radio. Her work has been placed in several international competitions.

Sylvia Fairley lives beside the Deben estuary in Suffolk. Having worked most of her life as a professional flautist, she now divides her time between music and writing.

Kate Foley's latest, *The Don't Touch Garden*, which re-visits issues about the gains and losses of adoption, is now out from Arachne Press. She's working towards a 2016 New and Selected from Shoestring Press.

Gabriel Griffin is creator and organiser of the Poetry on the Lake international events (poetryonthelake.org), poet and author. Her poems have appeared in many publications.

Joy Howard founded Grey Hen Press post retirement in 2007. She's in her mid-seventies but hasn't run out of steam yet.

Angela Kirby's poems are widely published. Her collections, *Mr. Irresistible, Dirty Work, A Scent of Winter* and *The Days After Always*, New and Selected Poems are all from Shoestring Press.

Pauline Kirk, poet and novelist, lives in York. Her latest novel, Border 7, was published by Stairwell Books in 2015. She also writes as PJ Quinn and edits Fighting Cock Press.

Wendy Klein is published in many magazines and journals She has two collections from Cinnamon Press: 'Cuba in the Blood' (2009) and 'Anything in Turquoise' (2014). A third collection is in the making.

Stevie Krayer's latest poetry publications are *New Monkey* (2014) and an anthology co-edited with R V Bailey *A Speaking Silence*: Quaker Poets of Today (2013), both from Indigo Dreams.

Gill Learner's poems are published widely. Her first collection, *The Agister's Experiment* (Two Rivers Press, 2011) sold well and a second, working title Chill Factor will appear in 2016.

Mandy Macdonald is Australian and lives in Aberdeen. Her poems have appeared most recently in *Outlook Variable* (Grey Hen Press 2014), *Word Bohemia, The Fat Damsel, Snakeskin, Clear Poetry*, and *The Stare's Nest*.

Alison Mace has always written poetry, more freely since her release from school-teaching. She lives in Gloucestershire

Char March lived near Berwick-upon-Tweed and used to watch the coble-netting of salmon. She's won awards for poetry, play writing and short fiction.Her five poetry collections include *The Thousand Natural Shocks* (Indigo Dreams 2011).
www.charmarch.co.uk

Jenny Morris writes poems and fiction. She lives in Norfolk. Her latest pamphlet is 'Keeping Secrets' (Cinnamon Press 2015).

Frances Nagle's publications are *Steeplechase Park* (Rockingham Press), *The War in Fraxinus Excelsior* and *You Can't Call a Hedgehog Hopscotch* (for children) from Dagger Press. She lives in Stockport.

Melanie Penycate teaches Psychology, has two published collections and work in reputable magazines and anthologies. She lives in West Sussex and has an MA in creative writing from Chichester University.

Katrina Porteous lives in Northumberland. Her collections include *The Lost Music* (Bloodaxe 1996) and *Two Countries* (Bloodaxe 2014).

Caroline Price is a violinist and teacher living and working in Kent. She has published short stories and three collections of poetry, most recently Wishbone (Shoestring Press 2008).

Eveline Pye spent eight years in Zambia working as a research analyst in the copper mining industry, and is now involved in fostering international links between mathematics and the arts.

Maggie Sawkins won the 2013 Ted Hughes Award for New Work in Poetry for her live literature production 'Zones of Avoidance'. She lives in Portsmouth where she organises *Tongues&Grooves*.

Vee Singleton now lives in rural Suffolk. An eclectic mix – gardener, walker, observer and occasional poet. Retired, though not from the aforementioned.

Ruth Smith has been writing poems for several years and has been published in several magazines and anthologies. She attends workshops and seminars run by The Poetry School.

Anne Stewart runs the poet showcase www.poetrypf.co.uk and is Administrator for Second Light network. She has won the Bridport Prize (2008) and published one collection, T*he Janus Hour*, (Oversteps Books, 2010).

Hannah Stone has an MA in Creative Writing and been published in several anthologies and journals, including online. Her first solo collection is forthcoming with Stairwell Books, York, in 2016.

Sheila Templeton is a prize winning Scottish poet. Her next full collection will be available in 2016 from Red Squirrel.

Deborah Sloan is a counsellor and creative writing facilitator, amateur flamenco dancer and avid baker. Glasgow born, she now lives in Sussex with her husband and a Siamese cat called Chico.

Jean Watkins lives near Reading. Her poems have appeared in many anthologies and magazines. Her collection Scrimshaw was published by Two Rivers Press in 2013.

Christine Webb's *After Babel*, published in 2004 by Peterloo, is now reprinted by Cinnamon Press, who also published her *Catching Your Breath* in 2011.

Lynne Wycherley lives near a headland in the West Country. She has an empathy for wild landscapes, and the creatures that inhabit them. *Her Listening to Light: new and selected poems* (2014) is available from Shoestring Press, Nottingham.

Joy Howard is the founder of Grey Hen Press, which specialises in publishing the work of older women poets.She has edited six previous full length Grey Hen Press anthologies and a series of chapbooks, and published a collection of her own poems *Exit Moonshine* (Grey Hen 2009) about her 'coming out' experiences in the 1980s. Her work has appeared in numerous anthologies and magazines and her second collection, Refurbishment, was published by Ward Wood in 2011.

Sue Hardy-Dawson is a poet, illustrator and artist, who has been widely published in children's poetry anthologies. She has a First Class Honours Degree and has provided workshops, both in schools and for the Foundation for Children and Arts. As a dyslexic poet,she is especially interested in breaking down barriers to creativity and encouraging reluctant readers and writers.

Acknowledgements

ANN ALEXANDER 'Bowerbird' *Nasty, British & Short* (Peterloo Poets 2007); ALISON BRACKENBURY 'Species' in anthologies *For Rhino in a Shrinking World* (The Poets Printery 2013) and *Zambia Grade 11 English Learner's Book* (Oxford University Press 2015); CAROLINE CARVER 'Dreaming the Ancestor' *Fish Eaters* (University of Plymouth Press 2015); DEBJANI CHATTERJEE 'The Elephant' *I Was That Woman* (Hippopotamus Press, 1989) and *Namaskar* (Redbeck Press 2004); ROSE COOK 'Buffalo' *Notes from a Bright Field* (Cultured Llama Publishing 2013); JULIA DEAKIN 'Lumbricus Rex' *Eleven Wonders* (Graft Poetry 2012); ANGELA KIRBY 'Poverty Pig' *A Scent of Winter* (Shoestring Press 2013); PAULINE KIRK 'Black Velvet' published as 'Mole' in *Quantum Leap*; GILL LEARNER 'A Bookworm Updates Itself' published in *Acumen*; JENNY MORRIS 'Fish Crow' *The Sin Eater* (Meon Valley Printers 1992); FRANCES NAGLE 'Amphibian Love Song' *Steeplechase Park*, Rockingham Press (1996); MELANIE PENYCATE 'Urbane Gorilla' *Feeding Humming Birds* (Oversteps 2009). First published in The North; KATRINA PORTEOUS 'Snail': excerpt from *Dunstanburgh*, first broadcast on BBC Radio 4 (2004) published by Smokestack Books 2004 and reprinted in *Two Countries* (Bloodaxe 2014); CAROLINE PRICE 'Foundling' *Wishbone* (Shoestring Press 2008); EVELINE PYE 'Walking Whales' *Smoke that Thunders* (Mariscat Press 2015). First published in *Orbis*; RUTH SMITH 'Watching Grass Snakes' in anthology *Her Wings of Glass* (Second Light Publications 2015); HANNAH STONE 'Doubletake' published online in *Caught in the Net*; JEAN WATKINS 'Shinglebacks' *Scrimshaw* (Two Rivers Press 2013), first published in *Magma*. CHRISTINE WEBB 'A Question of Balance' *After Babel* (Peterloo, 2004)